The UNITED STATES PRESIDENTS

★ John Quincy ★
ADAMS

Heidi M.D. Elston

Big Buddy Books
An Imprint of Abdo Publishing
abdopublishing.com

abdopublishing.com

Published by Abdo Publishing, a division of ABDO, PO Box 398166, Minneapolis, Minnesota 55439. Copyright © 2017 by Abdo Consulting Group, Inc. International copyrights reserved in all countries. No part of this book may be reproduced in any form without written permission from the publisher. Big Buddy Books™ is a trademark and logo of Abdo Publishing.

Printed in the United States of America, North Mankato, Minnesota
062016
092016

THIS BOOK CONTAINS
RECYCLED MATERIALS

Design: Sarah DeYoung, Mighty Media, Inc.
Production: Mighty Media, Inc.
Editor: Lauren Kukla
Cover Photograph: Getty Images
Interior Photographs: Alamy (pp. 11, 19, 27); Corbis (pp. 5, 7); Getty Images (pp. 7, 23, 29); Library of
    Congress (p. 25); Northwind (pp. 6, 9, 17, 21); Picture History (pp. 13, 15)

Cataloging-in-Publication Data

Names: Elston, Heidi M.D., author.
Title: John Quincy Adams / by Heidi M.D. Elston.
Description: Minneapolis, MN : Abdo Publishing, [2017] | Series: United States
    presidents | Includes bibliographical references and index.
Identifiers: LCCN 2015957271 | ISBN 9781680780826 (lib. bdg.) |
    ISBN 9781680775020 (ebook)
Subjects: LCSH: Adams, John Quincy, 1767-1848--Juvenile literature. |
    Presidents--United States--Biography--Juvenile literature. | United States--
    Politics and government--1825-1829--Juvenile literature.
Classification: DDC 973.5/5092 [B]--dc23
LC record available at http://lccn.loc.gov/2015957271

Contents

John Quincy Adams

John Quincy Adams was the sixth US president. He was the first president's son to become president. Adams's father, John Adams, was the second US president.

Adams served just one term as president. He fought for what he believed was right. Along the way, he made many **political** enemies.

Adams spent his life serving his country. His work helped change the nation for the better. Today, Adams is remembered as one of America's greatest **diplomats**.

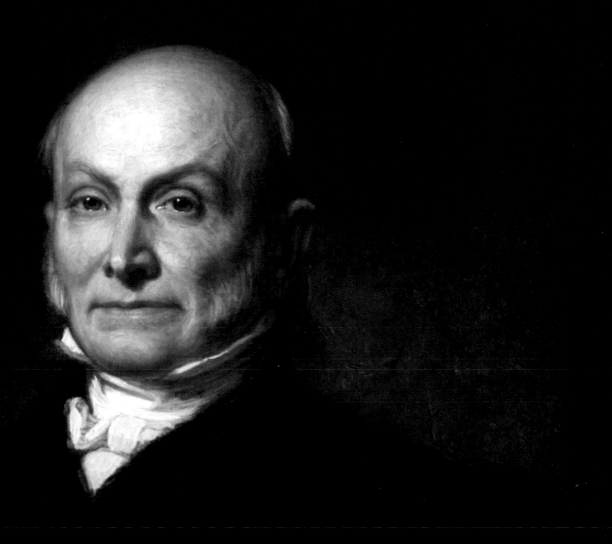

Timeline

1767

On July 11, John Quincy Adams was born in Braintree, Massachusetts.

1803

Adams was elected to the US Senate.

1817

President James Monroe made Adams **secretary of state**.

1825
On March 4, Adams became the sixth US president.

1841
Adams was a **lawyer** for the *Amistad* **captives**.

1830
Adams was elected to the US House of **Representatives**.

1848
On February 23, John Quincy Adams died.

Witnessing History

John Quincy Adams was born on July 11, 1767, in Braintree, Massachusetts. The town was later renamed Quincy. John Quincy's parents were John and Abigail Adams. As a child, John Quincy saw an early battle of the **American Revolution**.

★ FAST FACTS ★

Born: July 11, 1767

Wife: Louisa Catherine Johnson (1775–1852)

Children: four

Political Party: Democratic-Republican

Age at Inauguration: 57

Years Served: 1825–1829

Vice President: John C. Calhoun

Died: February 23, 1848, age 80

Abigail Adams

John Adams

During the war, John Quincy's parents provided most of his education. Then, in 1778, John went to Europe. John Quincy joined him. He lived throughout Europe for most of his teenage years.

In 1785, John Quincy returned to America. He entered Harvard College in Massachusetts. After college, John Quincy decided to study law.

In 1790, John Quincy became a **lawyer**. He also began writing **political** newspaper articles. President George Washington liked John Quincy's writings. Washington made him **minister** to the Netherlands.

John Quincy learned to
speak French and Dutch
while living in Europe.

Life in Europe

In 1794, Adams sailed to Europe to begin his new **career**. As **minister**, he reported to President Washington on events in European countries. Meanwhile, he married Louisa Catherine Johnson in 1797.

That same year, Adams became minister to Prussia. There, Mr. and Mrs. Adams's first son was born in 1801. Later that year, the family moved to Boston, Massachusetts. There, Adams briefly worked as a **lawyer**.

Adams met Louisa on a trip to London, England. He thought she was charming, warm, and well educated.

Senator Adams

Adams soon decided to work in **politics**. In 1802, he was elected to the Massachusetts state senate. The next year, he won election to the US Senate.

In 1807, President Thomas Jefferson called for a shipping **embargo**. Adams **supported** the president. However, this action made him unpopular in New England.

The next year, Adams quit the Senate. Then, in 1809, President James Madison gave Adams a new job. He was now **minister** to Russia.

Mr. and Mrs. Adams had three sons. A daughter died as a baby. Their younger sons were John (*left*) and Charles Francis (*below*).

Secretary Adams

By 1812, the nation was at war again. America and Great Britain were fighting each other in the **War of 1812**. In 1814, Adams helped make peace with the British. Then, Adams served as **minister** to Great Britain.

Adams returned to the United States in 1817. President James Monroe made him **secretary of state**. At that time, Spain owned the Florida Territory. Adams made a deal with Spanish leaders. Spain agreed to give Florida to the United States!

President James Monroe

A Close Election

In 1824, Adams decided to run for president. He was one of four men running. One **candidate** was war hero Andrew Jackson.

Jackson received 99 **electoral votes**. Adams had 84 votes. The other votes were split between the other men. To win, a candidate needed more than half the total votes. None of the men had enough.

★ DID YOU KNOW? ★

Throughout his presidency, Adams exercised every day. He also wrote daily in his diary.

John C. Calhoun originally ran for president. But he withdrew and became Adams's vice president instead.

According to the US **Constitution**, the House of **Representatives** now had to choose the president. The House chose from the top three **candidates**. Henry Clay had the least votes. That meant he was out of the race.

Clay decided to **support** Adams. With Clay's help, Adams was elected president in February 1825. Then, he chose Clay as his **secretary of state**.

Jackson's supporters in Congress were angry. They claimed Clay had helped Adams so they could both get into office. Now Adams had enemies in Congress.

PRESIDENT ADAMS'S CABINET

March 4, 1825–March 4, 1829

★ **STATE:** Henry Clay
★ **TREASURY:** Richard Rush
★ **WAR:** James Barbour,
   Peter B. Porter (from June 21, 1828)
★ **NAVY:** Samuel Lewis Southard
★ **ATTORNEY GENERAL:** William Wirt

Secretary of State Henry Clay

President Adams

President Adams wanted to make America better. He wanted to build new roads and waterways. He also wanted laws to **protect** Native Americans.

Congress refused most of Adams's ideas. In 1828, Adams signed a bill meant to protect New England factories. Northerners **supported** the bill. But Southerners were against it.

SUPREME COURT APPOINTMENTS ★

Robert Trimble: 1826

Adams is the first president of whom a photograph exists.

Another Election

Adams held little hope for reelection in 1828. This was one of the ugliest elections in US history. Once again, Adams ran against Andrew Jackson.

The campaign was hateful. Both sides took on **political** and personal attacks. Adams had too many political enemies to win the election. So, Jackson won.

Adams took his loss hard. He did not go to Jackson's **inauguration**. In 1829, Adams returned to Quincy.

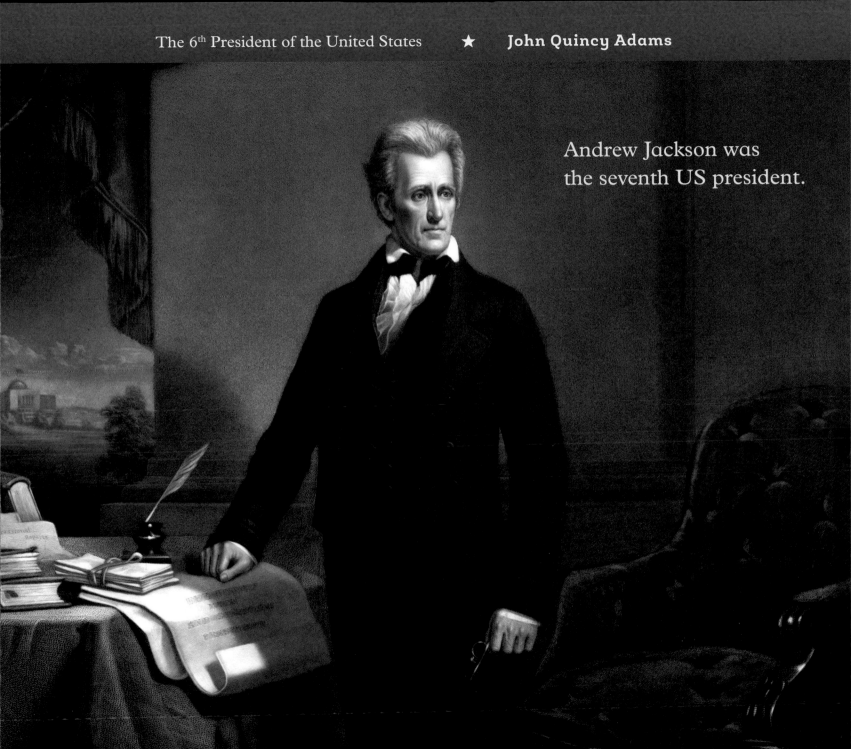

Andrew Jackson was the seventh US president.

Congressman

After his presidency, Adams planned to live quietly. But in 1830, he was elected to the US House of **Representatives**. He served in the House for the rest of his life.

In Congress, Adams fought slavery. Southern Congressmen passed several gag rules. They banned any talk of slavery in the House.

The gag rules kept laws against slavery from being passed. Adams fought the gag rules for eight years. Congress finally ended them in 1844.

Adams had not been a popular president. But he was well liked and respected in Congress.

In 1841, Adams worked on an important law case. Two years earlier, a group of **captive** Africans had been on the slave ship *Amistad*. The Africans took control of the ship.

After taking the ship, the Africans sailed to the United States. There, they were arrested. Adams became their **lawyer**. He fought for their freedom and won the case.

On February 23, 1848, John Quincy Adams died. He had earned the nation's respect. Adams is remembered as a great **diplomat**.

★ DID YOU KNOW? ★

Louisa Adams is the only first lady born outside of the United States. She was born in England.

Adams's diaries have given historians much information about his life.

Office of the President

Branches of Government

The US government has three branches. They are the executive, legislative, and judicial branches. Each branch has some power over the others. This is called a system of checks and balances.

★ Executive Branch

The executive branch enforces laws. It is made up of the president, the vice president, and the president's cabinet. The president represents the United States around the world. He or she also signs bills into law and leads the military.

★ Legislative Branch

The legislative branch makes laws, maintains the military, and regulates trade. It also has the power to declare war. This branch includes the Senate and the House of Representatives. Together, these two houses form Congress.

★ Judicial Branch

The judicial branch interprets laws. It is made up of district courts, courts of appeals, and the Supreme Court. District courts try cases. Sometimes people disagree with a trial's outcome. Then he or she may appeal. If a court of appeals supports the ruling, a person may appeal to the Supreme Court.

Qualifications for Office

To be president, a candidate must be at least 35 years old. The person must be a natural-born US citizen. He or she must also have lived in the United States for at least 14 years.

Electoral College

The US presidential election is an indirect election. Voters from each state choose electors. These electors represent their state in the Electoral College. Each elector has one electoral vote. Electors cast their vote for the candidate with the highest number of votes from people in their state. A candidate must receive the majority of Electoral College votes to win.

Term of Office

Each president may be elected to two four-year terms. The presidential election is held on the Tuesday after the first Monday in November. The president is sworn in on January 20 of the following year. At that time, he or she takes the oath of office.
It states:

> I do solemnly swear (or affirm) that I will faithfully execute the office of President of the United States, and will to the best of my ability, preserve, protect and defend the Constitution of the United States.

Line of Succession

The Presidential Succession Act of 1947 states who becomes president if the president cannot serve. The vice president is first in the line. Next are the Speaker of the House and the President Pro Tempore of the Senate. It may happen that none of these individuals is able to serve. Then the office falls to the president's cabinet members. They would take office in the order in which each department was created:

Secretary of State

Secretary of the Treasury

Secretary of Defense

Attorney General

Secretary of the Interior

Secretary of Agriculture

Secretary of Commerce

Secretary of Labor

Secretary of Health and Human Services

Secretary of Housing and Urban Development

Secretary of Transportation

Secretary of Energy

Secretary of Education

Secretary of Veterans Affairs

Secretary of Homeland Security

Benefits

★ While in office, the president receives a salary. It is $400,000 per year. He or she lives in the White House. The president also has 24-hour Secret Service protection.

★ The president may travel on a Boeing 747 jet. This special jet is called Air Force One. It can hold 70 passengers. It has kitchens, a dining room, sleeping areas, and more. Air Force One can fly halfway around the world before needing to refuel. It can even refuel in flight!

★ When the president travels by car, he or she uses Cadillac One. It is a Cadillac Deville that has been modified. The car has heavy armor and communications systems. The president may even take Cadillac One along when visiting other countries.

★ The president also travels on a helicopter. It is called Marine One. It may also be taken along when the president visits other countries.

★ Sometimes the president needs to get away with family and friends. Camp David is the official presidential retreat. It is located in Maryland. The US Navy maintains the retreat. The US Marine Corps keeps it secure. The camp offers swimming, tennis, golf, and hiking.

★ When the president leaves office, he or she receives lifetime Secret Service protection. He or she also receives a yearly pension of $203,700. The former president also receives money for office space, supplies, and staff.

PRESIDENTS AND THEIR TERMS

PRESIDENT	PARTY	TOOK OFFICE	LEFT OFFICE	TERMS SERVED	VICE PRESIDENT
George Washington	None	April 30, 1789	March 4, 1797	Two	John Adams
John Adams	Federalist	March 4, 1797	March 4, 1801	One	Thomas Jefferson
Thomas Jefferson	Democratic-Republican	March 4, 1801	March 4, 1809	Two	Aaron Burr, George Clinton
James Madison	Democratic-Republican	March 4, 1809	March 4, 1817	Two	George Clinton, Elbridge Gerry
James Monroe	Democratic-Republican	March 4, 1817	March 4, 1825	Two	Daniel D. Tompkins
John Quincy Adams	Democratic-Republican	March 4, 1825	March 4, 1829	One	John C. Calhoun
Andrew Jackson	Democrat	March 4, 1829	March 4, 1837	Two	John C. Calhoun, Martin Van Buren
Martin Van Buren	Democrat	March 4, 1837	March 4, 1841	One	Richard M. Johnson
William H. Harrison	Whig	March 4, 1841	April 4, 1841	Died During First Term	John Tyler
John Tyler	Whig	April 6, 1841	March 4, 1845	Completed Harrison's Term	Office Vacant
James K. Polk	Democrat	March 4, 1845	March 4, 1849	One	George M. Dallas
Zachary Taylor	Whig	March 5, 1849	July 9, 1850	Died During First Term	Millard Fillmore

PRESIDENT	PARTY	TOOK OFFICE	LEFT OFFICE	TERMS SERVED	VICE PRESIDENT
Millard Fillmore	Whig	July 10, 1850	March 4, 1853	Completed Taylor's Term	Office Vacant
Franklin Pierce	Democrat	March 4, 1853	March 4, 1857	One	William R.D. King
James Buchanan	Democrat	March 4, 1857	March 4, 1861	One	John C. Breckinridge
Abraham Lincoln	Republican	March 4, 1861	April 15, 1865	Served One Term, Died During Second Term	Hannibal Hamlin, Andrew Johnson
Andrew Johnson	Democrat	April 15, 1865	March 4, 1869	Completed Lincoln's Second Term	Office Vacant
Ulysses S. Grant	Republican	March 4, 1869	March 4, 1877	Two	Schuyler Colfax, Henry Wilson
Rutherford B. Hayes	Republican	March 3, 1877	March 4, 1881	One	William A. Wheeler
James A. Garfield	Republican	March 4, 1881	September 19, 1881	Died During First Term	Chester Arthur
Chester Arthur	Republican	September 20, 1881	March 4, 1885	Completed Garfield's Term	Office Vacant
Grover Cleveland	Democrat	March 4, 1885	March 4, 1889	One	Thomas A. Hendricks
Benjamin Harrison	Republican	March 4, 1889	March 4, 1893	One	Levi P. Morton
Grover Cleveland	Democrat	March 4, 1893	March 4, 1897	One	Adlai E. Stevenson
William McKinley	Republican	March 4, 1897	September 14, 1901	Served One Term, Died During Second Term	Garret A. Hobart, Theodore Roosevelt

PRESIDENT	PARTY	TOOK OFFICE	LEFT OFFICE	TERMS SERVED	VICE PRESIDENT
Theodore Roosevelt	Republican	September 14, 1901	March 4, 1909	Completed McKinley's Second Term, Served One Term	Office Vacant, Charles Fairbanks
William Taft	Republican	March 4, 1909	March 4, 1913	One	James S. Sherman
Woodrow Wilson	Democrat	March 4, 1913	March 4, 1921	Two	Thomas R. Marshall
Warren G. Harding	Republican	March 4, 1921	August 2, 1923	Died During First Term	Calvin Coolidge
Calvin Coolidge	Republican	August 3, 1923	March 4, 1929	Completed Harding's Term, Served One Term	Office Vacant, Charles Dawes
Herbert Hoover	Republican	March 4, 1929	March 4, 1933	One	Charles Curtis
Franklin D. Roosevelt	Democrat	March 4, 1933	April 12, 1945	Served Three Terms, Died During Fourth Term	John Nance Garner, Henry A. Wallace, Harry S. Truman
Harry S. Truman	Democrat	April 12, 1945	January 20, 1953	Completed Roosevelt's Fourth Term, Served One Term	Office Vacant, Alben Barkley
Dwight D. Eisenhower	Republican	January 20, 1953	January 20, 1961	Two	Richard Nixon
John F. Kennedy	Democrat	January 20, 1961	November 22, 1963	Died During First Term	Lyndon B. Johnson
Lyndon B. Johnson	Democrat	November 22, 1963	January 20, 1969	Completed Kennedy's Term, Served One Term	Office Vacant, Hubert H. Humphrey
Richard Nixon	Republican	January 20, 1969	August 9, 1974	Completed First Term, Resigned During Second Term	Spiro T. Agnew, Gerald Ford

PRESIDENT	PARTY	TOOK OFFICE	LEFT OFFICE	TERMS SERVED	VICE PRESIDENT
Gerald Ford	Republican	August 9, 1974	January 20, 1977	Completed Nixon's Second Term	Nelson A. Rockefeller
Jimmy Carter	Democrat	January 20, 1977	January 20, 1981	One	Walter Mondale
Ronald Reagan	Republican	January 20, 1981	January 20, 1989	Two	George H.W. Bush
George H.W. Bush	Republican	January 20, 1989	January 20, 1993	One	Dan Quayle
Bill Clinton	Democrat	January 20, 1993	January 20, 2001	Two	Al Gore
George W. Bush	Republican	January 20, 2001	January 20, 2009	Two	Dick Cheney
Barack Obama	Democrat	January 20, 2009	January 20, 2017	Two	Joe Biden

"**If your actions inspire others to dream more, learn more, do more, and become more, you are a leader.**" John Quincy Adams

★ WRITE TO THE PRESIDENT ★

You may write to the president at:
The White House
1600 Pennsylvania Avenue NW
Washington, DC 20500

You may e-mail the president at:
comments@whitehouse.gov

37

Glossary

American Revolution—the war between Americans and the British from 1775 to 1783. The Americans won their freedom from the British.

candidate (KAN-duh-dayt)—a person who seeks a political office.

captive—someone who is held as a prisoner or locked up.

career—a period of time spent in a certain job.

constitution (kahnt-stuh-TOO-shuhn)—the basic laws that govern a country or a state.

diplomat—someone who officially represents his or her country's government while in another country.

electoral vote—a vote cast by a member of the Electoral College for the candidate who received the most popular votes in his or her state.

embargo—a government order that bans something from happening.

inauguration (ih-naw-gyuh-RAY-shuhn)—a ceremony in which a person is sworn into office.

lawyer (LAW-yuhr)—a person who gives people advice on laws or represents them in court.

minister—a type of government official.

politics—the art or science of government. Something referring to politics is political. A person who is active in politics is a politician.

protect (pruh-TEHKT)—to guard against harm or danger.

representative—someone chosen in an election to act or speak for the people who voted for him or her.

secretary of state—a member of the president's cabinet who handles relations with other countries.

support—to believe in or be in favor of something.

War of 1812—a war between the United States and England from 1812 to 1815.

★ WEBSITES ★

To learn more about the US Presidents, visit **booklinks.abdopublishing.com**. These links are routinely monitored and updated to provide the most current information available.

Index